To d

MW01124402

Have fun!

GOTCHA!
WHATS IT?

Zinita Fowler
3-21-96

WHATS IT?

Collected by
ZINITA FOWLER

Illustrated by
Jack Fowler

PANDA BOOKS   ★   **Austin, Texas**

To all those students who
"got me"
through the years
and furnished the material
for these pages
I dedicate this book.

Library of Congress Cataloging-in-Publication Data

Fowler, Zinita.
  Gotcha! What's It
  Summary: Jokes designed to trick your friends by making them
feel just a little bit silly.
  1. Word games — Juvenile literature. [1. Jokes] I. Fowler, Jack, ill.
II. Title
GV1507.W8F68   1989   793.73   89-15981
ISBN 0-89015-936-X

REVISED EDITION

Copyright © 1993
By Zinita Fowler

Published in the United States of America
By Eakin Press
An Imprint of Sunbelt Media, Inc.
P.O. Drawer 90159   ★   Austin, TX 78709-0159

ISBN 0-89015-9367

Contents

Introduction

Let's say you are sitting in your room after school with your best friend. He has more or less showed you up in school that day, outspelling you in the spelling match and striking you out in the ballgame at recess. You need some kind of mild revenge.

So, you say to your friend, "I can prove you're not here."

Your friend says, "Are you nuts? Of course, I'm here, and you can't prove I'm not."

The following dialogue takes place:

You: Are you in New York City?

Friend: No.

You: Are you on the beach in Hawaii?

Friend: No.

You: Are you on a ski slope in Colorado?

Friend: No.

You: If you're not in any of those places, you must be someplace else, right?

Friend: Right.

You: And if you're someplace else, you can't be here.

Gotcha!

This kind of putting one over on someone else — one-upmanship the adults call it — has been the source of a lot of fun among kids for a long time. Some "gotchas" are so old, they're new again. At least one goes back to the days of Mother Goose. Try this one on your friends:

As I was going to St. Ives,
I met a man with seven wives,
Each wife had seven sacks,
Each sack had seven cats,
Each cat had seven kits,
Kits, cats, sacks, and wives,
How many were going to St. Ives?

(After your victims have racked their brains trying to add up all those sevens, tell them the answer is *one*. The person who was going to St. Ives *met* all these other things, which means they were headed in the opposite direction.)

In this book, you will find a large collection of "gotchas." To make them easier to find, they have been grouped along with others of the same kind. There should be enough here to make your friends start running when they see you coming. Or, more likely, they will seek you out to get in on the fun. So, ready, set, *Gotcha!*

You: Add these up:
1 ton of sawdust
1 ton of chewing gum
10 pounds of marshmallow
1 gallon of glue
A barrel of fat.
Now, have you got that in your head?
Friend: Yes.
You: I thought so!

Gotcha!

You: I bet I can make you say black.
Friend: I bet you can't.
You: What colors are in the American flag?
Friend: Red, white, and blue.
You: Aha! I told you I could make you say blue.
Friend: Oh, no . . . You said *black*.

Gotcha!

You: If you had on two shoes and just one sock, what else would you need?
Friend: A sock.
(So you sock him. But not too hard.)

Gotcha!

You: Spell too.
Friend: T-o-o.
You: Now, spell it another way.
Friend: T-w-o.
You: Now, spell twain.
Friend: T-w-a-i-n.
You: Now, say the three words.
Friend: Too, two, twain.
You: Great! When you get a little older, I'll teach you to say locomotive.

Gotcha!

2

You: Would you hit someone after he sur-
renders?
Friend: Of course not.
(Give your friend a sock on the arm; then,
before he can hit you back . . .)
You: I surrender!

Gotcha!

You: I saw an old dead rat. I one'd it.
Friend: I two'd it.
You: I three'd it.
Friend: I four'd it.
You: I five'd it.
Friend: I six'ed it.
You: I seven'd it.
Friend: I eight (ate) it.
(If your friend is on to this one, he may say, "I jumped
over it, and you eight it." Otherwise . . .)

Gotcha!

You: Three little monkeys sat in a tree,
Their names were Do and Re and Mi.
Do and Re fell off, so who was left?
Friend: Mi.

Gotcha!

You: Can you spell joke?
Friend: J-o-k-e.
You: Can you spell folk?
Friend: F-o-l-k.
You: Can you spell poke?
Friend: P-o-k-e.
You: Now, spell the white of an egg.
Friend: Y-o-l-k.
You: Wrong! The white of an egg is the albumin.

Gotcha!

3

You: Do you collect stamps?

Friend: No.

(You stamp on his foot — not too hard.)

You: Well, there's one to get you started.

If your friend replies: Yes

(You stamp on his foot — not too hard.)

You: There's another one for your collection.

Gotcha! Either way.

You: I have a friend who collects snakes. He has a python, a garter snake, and a hammerfer.

Friend: What's a hammerfer?

You: To hit nails with, dummy!

Gotcha!

You: I have a story to tell, but you have to help me. Every time I finish a sentence, you have to say, "Just like me."

Friend: Okay. (This is a very gullible friend.)

You: Once upon a time, I went out of my house for a walk.

Friend: Just like me.

You: I turned right at the corner and headed toward town.

Friend: Just like me.

You: I waited for the light to change and crossed the street.

Friend: Just like me.

You: I reached the corner in front of the big department store.

Friend: Just like me.

You: I saw a big crowd gathered there.

Friend: Just like me.

You: I pushed through the crowd to see what was happening.
Friend: Just like me.
You: There, in the middle of the crowd, was an old organ grinder, and he had a little monkey on a chain.
Friend: Just like me.

Gotcha!

You are walking along with your friend, and suddenly, you jump to one side.
You: Look out! There's a henweigh!
Friend: What's a henweigh?
You: Oh, about three pounds.

Gotcha!

You: If your forehead is a rooster, and your nose is a pullet, and your chin is a hen, can you remember which is which?
Friend: Sure. That's easy.
You: What did I say your nose was?
Friend: Pullet.
(So you pull it. But not too hard.)

Gotcha!

You: Ask me if I'm a boat.
Friend: Okay. Are you a boat?
You: Yes. Now, ask me if I'm a train.
Friend: Are you a train?
You: Certainly not. I just told you I'm a boat.

Gotcha!

You: Railroad crossing, look out for the cars. Can you spell that without any "r's"?
Friend: No. It's loaded with "r's."
You: Not really. I asked you to spell "that."

Gotcha!

5

You: Pete and Repeat were sitting on a log. Pete fell off. Who was left?

Friend: Repeat.

You: Pete and Repeat were sitting on a log. Pete fell off. Who was left?

(Keep this up until your friend catches on.)

Gotcha!

You: Adam and Eve and Pinch-me-quick
Went down to swim in a tank;
Adam and Eve just jumped right in,
So who was left on the bank?

Friend: Pinch-me-quick.

(So you pinch him, quick! But not too hard.)

Gotcha!

You: I have a riddle for you. What's high and white and cold with a peak on top and ears?

Friend: I don't know.

You: A mountain, of course. It's high and has a peak and the snow on it is white and cold.

Friend: But what about the ears?

You: Do you mean to tell me you never heard of mountaineers?

Gotcha!

You: If frozen water is iced water, what is frozen ink?

Friend: Iced ink. (Sounds like "I stink.")

You: I agree.

Gotcha!

You: I have a friend who's very sick. He has snoo in his blood.

Friend: What's snoo?

You: Oh, nothing much. What's new with you?

Gotcha!

You: We're very good friends, aren't we?

Friend: Yes.

You: Will you always remember me after we grow up?

Friend: Sure, I will.

You: Will you remember me after we get married?

Friend: Sure.

You: Will you remember me after we have children?

Friend: Yes.

You: Will you remember me after we have grandchildren?

Friend: Of course.

You: Will you remember me when I'm old and gray?

Friend: Yes.

You: Knock! Knock!

Friend: Who's there?

You: (with a big sigh) You've forgotten me already!

Gotcha!

You: I know someone who thinks he's an owl.

Friend: Who?

You: Now I know *two* people who think they're owls.

Gotcha!

You: When they take out your appendix, what do they call it?

Friend: An appendectomy.

You: Right. When they take out your tonsils, what do they call it?

Friend: A tonsillectomy.

7

You: Right. When they remove a growth from your head, what do they call it?

Friend: I don't know.

You: A haircut!

Gotcha!

You: What has more legs, one dog or no dog?

Friend: One dog, of course.

You: Wrong. No dog has eight legs, and that's more.

Gotcha!

You: If you decided to paper your house, could you put the paper on yourself?

Friend: Sure.

You: Don't you think it would be better if you put it on the wall?

Gotcha!

You: Which hand do you use when you stir the sugar in your tea?

Friend: My right (or possibly, my left.)

You: Yuck! How sloppy can you get? I stir my tea with a spoon.

Gotcha!

You: If two is company, and three is a crowd, what are four and five?

Friend: (thinks awhile) I don't know.

You: Nine, of course. Didn't you ever learn how to add?

Gotcha!

You: Do you know how many dead people are buried out there in the city cemetery?
Friend: Of course not. How many?
You: *All* of them. I hope.
Gotcha!

You: My dog can jump higher than the Empire State Building.
Friend: No he can't.
You: Sure, he can. The Empire State Building can't jump.
Gotcha!

You: A man just moved in next door to us who has asparagus growing out of his ears.
Friend: Yuck. How did that happen?
You: He doesn't know. He told me he planted peanuts.
Gotcha!

You: There are many ways of making money, but only one honest way.
Friend: Oh, yeah? What's that?
You: I was pretty sure you wouldn't know.
Gotcha!

You: What has eighteen legs, little red eyes, and a long stinger?
Friend: I don't know.
You: Neither do I. But there's one crawling up the sleeve of your shirt.
Gotcha!

9

You: If twelve make a dozen, how many make a million?

Friend: Beats me. (This is a rather dumb friend.)

You: Not many.

Gotcha!

You: What do you have to know before you start to teach your dog some tricks?

Friend: What?

You: More than the dog.

Gotcha!

You: Can you spell blind pig?

Friend: Sure, that's easy. B-l-i-n-d p-i-g.

You: Wrong. You spell it b-l-n-d p-g. If you leave in the two eyes (i's), the pig wouldn't be blind.

Gotcha!

You: If a rooster says, "Cock-a-doodle-do" and Uncle Sam says, "Yankee Doodle Do," what does your old maid sister say?

Friend: Tell me.

You: "Any dude'll do!"

Gotcha!

You: My bike has no wheels or pedals. All it has is a horn.

Friend: How does it go?

You: Beep! Beep!

Gotcha!

You: Can you carry a tune?

Friend: Certainly.

You: Then carry the one you've just been singing out into the backyard and bury it!

Gotcha!

You: I can prove that animals are smarter than people.
Friend: How?
You: If fifteen horses run a race, thousands of people pay to see it. If fifteen people ran a race, not one horse would go.

Gotcha!

You: Want to hear a couple of dillies?
Friend: Sure.
You: Dilly, dilly.

Gotcha!

You: What three words do stupid people use more than any other?
Friend: I don't know.
You: Right!

Gotcha!

You: If an Eskimo from the North Pole says, "Blub, blub," what would an Eskimo from the South Pole say?
Friend: Beats me.
You: "Blub, blub, youall."

Gotcha!

You: I've been weighing myself on scales that give out those little cards with your weight on them. I started out weighing 95 pounds and now I weigh 110.
Friend: Gosh! You've gained a lot of weight.

11

You: Not really. You see, I have all these little cards in my pocket.

Gotcha!

You: I'm homesick.
Friend: But you live at home.
You: Yeah, and I'm sick of it.

Gotcha!

You: I have three words of advice for you. Don't argue.
Friend: That's only two.
You: You've started already!

Gotcha!

You: Have you met my parents?
Friend: No.
You: (sticking out your hand) Then, meet my paw.

Gotcha!

You: I will tell your fortune. For just a dollar, I will answer any two questions you ask me.
Friend: Well, okay. (Hands over the dollar.) But don't you think a dollar is a lot for just two questions?
You: Yes, I do. Now, what is your other question?

Gotcha!

You: This morning, I fell off a 100-foot ladder.
Friend: Good grief! Weren't you hurt?
You: No. I was just on the first rung when I fell.

Gotcha!

You: I'll give you five bucks to do my worrying for me.
Friend: That's a deal. Where's the five bucks?
You: That's your first worry.

Gotcha!

You: I wish I had enough money to buy an elephant.
Friend: What in the world do you want with an elephant?
You: I don't want an elephant. I just want enough money to buy one.

Gotcha!

You: I fell over twenty feet today.
Friend: Were you hurt?
You: Oh, no. I was just late getting to my seat at the theater.

Gotcha!

You: I got a new dog today.
Friend: What kind is he?
You: He's a Mexican spitz.
Friend: I never heard of that kind of dog.
You: He's very rare. Instead of barking, he goes, "Patooie, olé! Patooie, olé!"

Gotcha!

You: I'm really tired.
Friend: Why? What did you do today?
You: A lot. My heart beat 3,283 times, my blood traveled 168 miles, and I breathed 2,340 times. I inhaled 438 cubic feet of air, ate three pounds of food, drank two quarts of liquid. I moved 750 muscles, spoke thousands of words, and generated 450 tons of energy. My nails and hair both grew, and I exercised 7,000,000 brain cells. I'm exhausted.

(If your friend thinks fast on his feet, he can turn the "gotcha" on you by saying, "I believe all of that but the last statement.")

Gotcha!

You: Well, I guess I won't be playing checkers with Bill anymore.
Friend: Why not?
You: Would you play a game with a guy who cheats and moves his checkers when you're not looking?
Friend: No, I wouldn't.
You: Neither would Bill.

Gotcha!

You: Did you know that I play on the football team?
Friend: Oh, yeah? What position?
You: Oh, sort of crouched down and bent over.

Gotcha!

You: Did you know there's going to be only a half-day of school this morning?
Friend: Hooray! Let's go out and do something.
You: Can't. There's going to be another half-day this afternoon.

Gotcha!

You: What do you call that stuff that grows on the outside of a tree?
Friend: Bark.
You: What?
Friend: Bark! Bark!
You: Oh, well, if you insist. Bow-wow! Bow-wow!

Gotcha!

14

You: I read in the paper about a guy who came to this country from overseas and knew only three words of English, but he was rich in a couple of years.

Friend: That's hard to believe. What were the three words?

You: "Stick 'em up!"

Gotcha!

You: (on a hot day) Is your air conditioner running?

Friend: Yes.

You: You'd better go and stop it before it gets away.

Gotcha!

Friend: May I join you?

You: Gosh, am I falling apart?

Gotcha!

You: We just got rid of that noise in the back of the car.

Friend: What did you do, take it to the garage?

You: Naw. My dad made my little sister sit up front.

Gotcha!

You: Can you change a quarter for me?

Friend: Sure.

You: Good. Change it into a dollar.

Gotcha!

You: You'd be a really great dancer except for two things.

Friend: Oh, yeah? And what are those?

You: Your feet.

Gotcha!

You: I was born in Texas.
Friend: What part?
You: *All* of me.

Gotcha!

You: I hear that fish is brain food.
Friend: Good. I eat it all the time.
You: There goes another theory down the drain!

Gotcha!

You: Say, can I borrow your pen?
Friend: Sure.
You: Got a piece of writing paper I can use?
Friend: Right here.
You: Going past the post office on your way home?
Friend: I always do.
You: Wait 'til I finish writing this note, okay?
Friend: Okay.
You: Can you lend me a stamp?
Friend: I guess so.
You: Thanks. Now, what's your girlfriend's address?

Gotcha!

You: Whew! I've just been in a terrible fight.
Friend: Who won?
You: I don't know. I left in the middle of it.

Gotcha!

(Your friend has scratched his arm, and you are giving him first aid.)
You: Does this alcohol make your arm smart?
Friend: Sure does.
You: Want me to rub some on your head?

Gotcha!

16

You: Do you know the best way to avoid biting insects?
Friend: How?
You: When you see a bug coming your way, just keep your mouth closed.
Gotcha!

You: When I get rich, I'm going to have three swimming pools: one with cold water, one with warm water, and one with no water at all.
Friend: Why would you want a pool with no water in it?
You: For my friends who can't swim, of course.
Gotcha!

You: I betcha I can jump across the street.
Friend: You're crazy. No one can jump that far.
You: I can. I'll bet you a quarter.
Friend: You're on.
(You walk calmly across the street, and once you're on the other side, jump up and down like crazy.)
Gotcha!

Friend: Lend me a quarter. I need to call my friend.
You: Here's fifty cents. Call *all* your friends.
Gotcha!

You: Want a roast beef sandwich?
Friend: Sure.
You: Do you want me to make the meat lean?
Friend: Yes.
You: To the left or to the right?
Gotcha!

You: (in an offhanded way) You know something?
Friend: No. What?
You: Boy, are you dumb!
Gotcha!

You: Be sure to keep your eyes open tomorrow.
Friend: Why?
You: Because you'll bump into everything if you don't.
Gotcha!

You: I have a headache.
Friend: What are you taking for it?
You: What'll you give me?
Gotcha!

You: Between my dad and me, we know everything.
Friend: Oh, yeah?
You: Yeah. Ask me something.
Friend: Okay. What's the population of New York City?
You: That's one of the things my dad knows.
Gotcha!

You: Just between you and me, don't you think kissing is kind of silly?
Friend: Oh, I don't know about that.
You: Aw, come on. Between you and me, kissing would be absolutely ridiculous!
Gotcha!

You: Boy, have I got a toothache!
Friend: I'd have that tooth pulled if it were mine.
You: So would I — if it were yours.
Gotcha!

You: How many peas in a pint?

18

Friend: I don't know. A lot, I guess.

You: Only one. *P*-i-n-t. Now, how many peas go in a pot?

Friend: You won't get me again. Only one. *P*-o-t.

You: Wrong. None. Peas won't go in a pot. You have to put them in.

Gotcha!

You: How much do you suppose a donkey weighs?

Friend: I have no idea.

You: Hop on those scales over there and we'll find out.

Gotcha!

"GOTCHAS" TO ACT OUT

These "Gotchas" are different from the ones in the first section in that they require a bit of preparation and usually an accomplice or two. They can be used as party gags or as between-act entertainment at programs.

The Secret Society

You ask for volunteers who would like to become members of a Secret Society. When you get two or three volunteers, line them up in front of everyone. Then, you say:

"This is a very ancient and honorable society, and the initiation ceremony must be done with seriousness and dignity. Now, stand up straight and place the palms of your hands together at chest level. Repeat the words of the initiation after me, and each time you say a word, bow at the waist.

"Oo-wah." (Victims repeat, bowing at the waist.)

"Ta-goo." (Ditto.)

"Si-am." (Again.)

"Now, say all three words, bowing at the waist with each word." (Victims say, "Oo-wah, Ta-goo, Si-am.")

"Say it again, faster." (Continue, until victims realize they are saying "Ooh, what a goose I am!")

!!!!

A Running Gag

You will need three friends to help you. They are lined up side by side in front of everyone. Ask for a volunteer who is a good runner. (This is a neat trick to play on someone who has a big head because of his running ability.)

When you have your victim, give these instructions:

"Pretend these are three trees in the forest. You have an axe in your hand. Run around the trees and give one of them a whack behind the knees with your imaginary axe. If you do it right, he will fall down. Run around the trees again and give the second tree a whack behind the knees. He should fall down too. Do the same thing with the third tree, and he will fall. Then, continue running around the trees until I tell you to stop."

(The victim will usually do as instructed, with perhaps a false start or two until he gets it right.)

After the trees are down and the victim is still running, you say, "This little drama only goes to prove that even after the trees are down, the sap keeps running."

!!!!

A Fishing Trip

This trick requires the help of one friend and a long piece (about ten feet or more) of heavy twine. You hold up one end of the twine and your friend holds up the other.

You say: "We need some volunteers to help us out with this stunt." (As victims hold up their hands, instruct them, one at a time, to come up and take hold of the twine with their right hands.)

When you have four or five, this is the dialogue:

Friend: Where've you been?
You: Oh, I been fishin' down at the creek.
Friend: Fish biting pretty good?
You: Yeah, pretty good.
Friend: Catch anything?
You: Not much. Just a few suckers.

!!!!

Ugly Face

Two friends will be needed for this trick. You are more or less the director. They are seated in chairs, facing the group. Ask for a volunteer to help with the stunt. You give him his instructions privately, since only your friends and you should know what to expect.

The victim is given a very ugly Halloween mask.

22

You tell him to put it on and sneak up behind the two friends seated in chairs. Then, he is to suddenly thrust the ugly face at them, from the back, from the sides, anywhere to get a reaction from them. Your friends have been instructed to give no notice of the ugly face at all, no matter what the victim may try. They must maintain a serious, stoical expression.

Finally, the victim gives up and takes off the mask. *Then,* the two friends scream in terror at the sight of his real face, and run from the room.

!!!!

The Moonlight Night

An attractive girl is needed for this stunt. She knows her lines in advance, but the victim will be told what to say.

They stroll together out in front of the group, as if taking a walk. This is the dialogue:

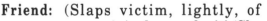

Victim: Some night!
Friend: Some night.
Victim: Some stars!
Friend: Some stars.
Victim: Some moon!
Friend: Some moon.
Victim: Some dew!
Friend: (Slaps victim, lightly, of course.) And some don't! (She walks off the stage.)

!!!!

Hard of Hearing

You will need two plastic bananas attached to a headband so they look as if they are in your ears. A friend will wear this device since once again you will be the director. Your friend is seated in front of the group. The victim is instructed to ask your friend why he has bananas in his ears. The friend ignores him, as if he doesn't know he is there. The victim is instructed to continue to ask why the bananas are there. At last, your friend notices the victim.

He says: "Oh, I'm sorry. I couldn't hear what you were saying. You see, I have these bananas in my ears."

!!!!

The Captured Thing

Your friend walks out in front of everyone, hands cupped together as if he is holding something in them.

He says to the victim: "Guess what I have in my hands."

The victim has been instructed to try to guess what your friend may have in his hands. He might guess a rock, a flower, a bug — anything logical.

Friend: (each time, shaking his head) Larger.

The victim then guesses some larger items, like a ball, a picture, an eraser, etc. Each time your friend shakes his head. If the victim wants to give up, you encourage him to continue. Finally, he will guess something outrageous, like a horse.

Friend: (peeking into his hands) What color?

!!!!

The Railroad Track

The victim is to act as the railroad agent. You may have as many as six or eight accomplices in this trick, one to act as the mother and the rest as children.

Mother: (approaching the agent) Oh, Mr. Agent, can you tell me what time the train from the north gets here?

Agent: (improvising) It gets here at 2:05 P.M.

Mother: (turning to child behind her) It gets here at 2:05 P.M.

1st Child: (turning to child next to him) It gets here at 2:05 P.M.

This is repeated, with each child in turn relaying to the child next to him the time the train is to arrive.

Mother: Mr. Agent, could you tell me what time the train from the south gets here?

Agent: It arrives at 2:30 P.M.

Mother: (turning to child behind her) It arrives at 2:30 P.M.

The same procedure is repeated as before, with each child telling the child next to him.

The mother then inquires about the train from the east, and the train from the west, with the repetition down the line to each child.

Mother: Mr. Agent, can you tell me what time it is now?

Agent: (has been instructed to name a time some distance removed from any of the train arrival times) It's 10:00 A.M., ma'am.

Information is repeated down the line.

Agent: Excuse me, ma'am, can you tell me what train you wish to catch?

Mother: Oh, we're not going to ride the train. (Yells to children) Come on, kids, it's safe to cross the tracks now.

!!!!

The Bakery

You are seated in a chair, pantomiming as if you are speaking into a phone.

You: Hello. Hello. Is this the bakery shop? I would like to place an order for a special cake. I want it made to look exactly like my car. That's right, my car. My car is bright yellow, with blue wheels and white side-walled tires. It's a sedan, four-door, with chrome trim along the sides. Do you think you can do that? Fine. And can you have it ready by tomorrow? Good. Good-bye.

The victim is the baker. It is the next day in his shop. As you enter, he pretends to set a cake down on the counter.

You: Ah, that's lovely. You have done a marvelous job. (Inspect the cake closely, then cry out in dismay) Oh! Oh, dear! This won't do, not at all!

Baker: What's the trouble?

You: My car is a Buick, and you've made the cake with a Chrysler body. That's all wrong. I'm sorry.

Baker: If you really want the cake, we can change it.

You: You can do that? How long will it take?

Baker: Several hours. Can you come back tomorrow?

You: Oh, yes. Thank you. Thank you very much!

The next day, you enter the shop again. The baker again brings out the cake.

You: Ah, that's just right. It's perfect this time.

Baker: Good. We worked on it most of the night. Where would you like me to deliver the cake?

You: I don't want it delivered. I'll eat it right here.

[Note: Certain scenes or passages of time can be shown with placards or by an announcer coming out and saying, "The Bakery Shop" or "The next day," etc.]

!!!!

Quickies

1. Select a volunteer wearing a coat. Ask him to come up front. Say: "I'll bet you can't button up your coat in a minute." The victim is sure he can. Say, "Go!" Time him. The coat will probably be buttoned in less than a minute, but chances are, the victim will have buttoned his coat *down* instead of *up*. Most people do.

!!!!

2. Ask for a volunteer to come to the front. Hold out your hand, facing him, fingers spread wide apart so all can see. Point to your pinky and say, "This is the baby."

Point to your ring finger and say, "Mother says, 'Don't touch the baby.'" Point to your middle finger and say, "Daddy says, 'Don't touch the baby.'" Point to your pointer finger and say, "Sister says, 'Don't touch the baby.'" Point to your thumb and say, "Brother says, 'Don't touch the baby.'" Then, ask the victim, "Now, which one did I say was the baby?" When the victim touches your pinky, slap his hand away and say, "Don't touch the baby!"

!!!!

3. For this stunt, you may select one or several volunteers. You say: "I am going to show you a simple little exercise. I'll bet you can't do it *exactly* as I do."

This is the exercise: Hold your left hand out in front of you, fingers spread apart. As you touch the tips of your fingers with the pointer finger of your right hand, you say: "Tommy, Tommy, Tommy, Tommy, Whoopee (here you slide your finger down the left side of your left pointer finger and up the right side of your thumb) Tommy. (Touch thumb. Reverse directions and go back, touching the tips of thumb and fingers again.) Tommy, Tommy, Tommy, Tommy, Tom." Inconspicuously, as though it is just a natural action, fold your arms when you are finished.

After a few tries, your victims will get the "Tommy" part of the exercise right, but very seldom will one fold his arms when finished. That's the "gotcha."

!!!!

4. Ask your volunteer to come to the front. Have him point to his head and say, aloud, the abbreviation of mountain.

Victim: "MT" (empty).

Ask him to cradle his chin in his hands and blink his eyes, rapidly, as if flirting, and say the abbreviation of quart.

27

Victim: "QT" (cutie).

!!!!

5. You come out onto the stage and begin making motions as if you are scatter-sowing seeds all around. The victim has been told what to say. He watches you for a while.

    Victim: What are you doing?

    You: I'm putting out elephant repellent in my yard.

    Victim: Don't be silly. There aren't any elephants around here.

    You: Yeah, I know. Works real well, doesn't it?

!!!!

6. The victim is a traveler, and you are a farmer.

    Victim: Can you tell me the way to Big Sandy?

    You: I'm afraid I don't know.

    Victim: Do you know the way to Edgewood?

    You: Nope.

    Victim: Then, could you tell me how to get to Dallas?

    You: Sure can't.

    Victim: You don't know much, do you?

    You: Nope. But I ain't lost.

!!!!

7. You will be the judge in this "gotcha" and will need four people to help you: one accomplice and three volunteers. The volunteers will be told the line they are to say.

    Judge: You boys have been brought to me because you caused a big commotion at the zoo today. Now, I want you to tell me your names and what you did.

    1st volunteer: My name is Henry, and I threw peanuts to the elephants.

28

2nd volunteer: My name is Sam, and I threw peanuts to the elephants.

3rd volunteer: My name is Pete, and I threw peanuts to the elephants.

Accomplice: (in a shaky voice) My name is Peanuts.

!!!!

8. You walk out in front with some pieces of notebook paper and some scissors, and start cutting the paper into pieces. A volunteer comes up to you.

Volunteer: What are you doing?

You: I'm playing hooky.

Volunteer: I mean what are you doing making a mess with that paper?

You: I told you. I'm playing hooky. I go to a correspondence school, and I'm cutting classes.

!!!!

9. This is a solo act. You appear onstage before the group, and say: I am the fastest quick-draw artist in the world. I can draw my gun and put it back into the holster so fast you can hardly see me do it. Want to see my quick draw?

Audience: Yeah!

You strike the traditional pose of the gunfighter, legs spread apart, knees bent, hands at the side of imaginary holsters.

You: Ready. Here's my quick draw. (You do absolutely nothing.) Want to see it again?

!!!!

10. Ask for a volunteer to play the part of the ticket seller at the movies. Your accomplices will be children who wish to go to the movie, but don't have the price of a ticket.

29

1st child: How much does it cost to get in?

Ticket seller: Fifty cents each.

1st child: Boy, I really want to see that movie, but I only have thirty-five cents.

2nd child: I only have a dime.

(Some ad-libbing among the children about wanting to see the movie and not having enough money. You are off to one side, watching and listening.)

You: (to children) You guys really want to see that movie, don't you?

Children: (together, various answers) Yeah! Sure do!

You: (to ticket seller) Count these kids as they go in.

(Happy children file past ticket seller, who counts them as they go by.)

You: (after last child has gone inside) How many did you get?

Ticket seller: I counted twelve.

You: Good. I was right. That's how many I counted too. Goodbye. (Wave to the ticket seller and leave the stage.)

!!!!

11. Announce that you need a volunteer to learn a new magic act. When your victim comes up on the stage, give him a kitchen match that has been struck and can no longer catch on fire. Tell him to break the match in the middle, not completely through, and hold it out in front of him, one end of the match in each hand.

You: Now, stomp the floor three times with your right foot.

(The victim stomps the floor as instructed, still holding the match.)

You: Stomp the floor again, three times.

(The victim does it again — and a few more times, if he seems willing to do it.)

You: (finally, with exaggerated sympathy) What's the matter, buddy? Won't your motorcycle start?

!!!!

12. You hold up a piece of paper and tell the audience: I have written down what you will do when I ask you a question. I need a volunteer who doesn't believe I know.

When the volunteer comes up on stage, ask him to give you the definition of either a goatee or an accordion.

After he has done so, show him that you have written on the paper: You can't tell me what a goatee (or accordion) is without using your hands. (This is true. It is virtually impossible. Most people will make a little pointing motion at their chins to define goatee, and will move their hands in and out to define accordion. If you happen to get one of the rare ones who does not, the "gotcha" is on you!)

!!!!

"GOTCHAS" TO THINK ABOUT

These "gotchas" are good to try on your "motor-mouth" friends who tend to operate the voice before the brain is in gear. They have logical, even visible answers sometimes. You will gain your "gotcha" by the way you ask the question, minimizing the "give-away word" in some instances, and insisting that there *is* a sensible answer to seemingly impossible questions in others.

No dialogue will be suggested, since the answers of the victims will vary from "Are you nuts?" to "I don't know," with many variations in between.

You are the driver of a bus. On your early morning run, you make six stops. At the first stop, ten people get on. At the second stop, three people get off and four people get on. At the third stop, six people get off and nine people get on. At the fourth stop, no one gets off, but four people get on. At the fifth stop, seven people get off and no one gets on. The sixth stop is the turnaround point. What is the name of the bus driver? (The key word in this "gotcha" is *you*. If you are the driver of a bus, *the name of the bus driver is the victim's name.* Most people will be so busy adding and subtracting passengers that they will fail to catch the key word.)

? ? ? ?

If a plane crashes right on the border between Canada and the United States, in which country will they bury the survivors? (They don't bury the *survivors*.)

? ? ? ?

It took five men one day to dig up a field.
How long will it take ten men to dig up the same field? (No time at all. The five men have already done the job.)

? ? ? ?

33

A young girl has gotten herself into a predicament. Somehow, she is shut up in a room made out of thick galvanized iron. There is a door, but no doorknob and only a keyhole with no key. There are no windows. In the room is a piano, an apple, a butcher knife, and a baseball bat. The girl escapes from the room. How? (There are five answers, and maybe more: 1. She took a key from the piano and opened the door. 2. She cut the apple in two with the knife. Two halves make a whole (hole) and she crawled out. 3. She picked up the baseball bat and struck three times. Three strikes and she's *out*. 4. She started to run around and around and around the room until she was all worn *out*. 5. She broke out with the measles.)

? ? ? ?

You are in a very strange house. It is perfectly square, but all sides of it face the south. If a bear walks past the window, what color is he? (Any house with all four sides facing south would have to be at the North Pole. Therefore, any bear that walked past would be a polar bear, and he would be white.)

? ? ? ?

What's the difference between an orange and a head of cabbage? (If you don't know, I'd certainly hate to send you to the grocery store!)

? ? ? ?

If one horse is shut up in a stable and another one is running down the road, which one would be singing, "Don't Fence Me In?" (Neither one. Horses can't sing!)

? ? ? ?

34

Mr. Jones is a butcher. He is six feet tall and wears a size twelve shoe. What does he weigh? (Meat, of course.)
? ? ? ?

If Washington's wife went to Wyoming while Washington's washerwoman worked hard to wash Washington's woolen workshirts, how many "w's" are there in all? (None. There are no "w's" in *all*.)
? ? ? ?

What month has twenty-eight days? (*All* of them.)
? ? ? ?

What does a baby chicken become after it is five days old? (Six days old.)
? ? ? ?

If you jumped into the Indian Ocean, what would you become? (All wet. You must have jumped in recently.)
? ? ? ?

If you were walking through the woods, would you rather have a lion eat you or a bear? (I'd rather have the lion eat the bear, of course.)
? ? ? ?

A novice farmer wrote the following letter to the Department of Agriculture: "Gentlemen: Something seems to be wrong with my chickens. Every morning when I go out into the farmyard, I find two or three of them on the ground, cold and stiff with their feet in the air. Can you please tell me what is the matter?" If you were writing the reply for the

Department of Agriculture, what would you say? (Dear sir: Your chickens are dead.)
? ? ? ?

Pick any year you wish, and tell me off the top of your head how many gallons of gasoline were exported from the United States in that year. (Your victim will protest that it's impossible; he'd have to look it up. The answer is quite simple. 1492 — None.)
? ? ? ?

What's the death rate in Albuquerque, New Mexico? (Same as everywhere. One to a person.)
? ? ? ?

How can three monstrously fat men walk under one umbrella and not get wet? (It isn't raining.)
? ? ? ?

Have many big men been born in the state of Maine? (Nope. Just little babies.)
? ? ? ?

What is the hardest train to catch? (They're all about the same if you let them get a head start.)
? ? ? ?

If there are 12 one-cent stamps in a dozen, how many four-cent stamps in a dozen? (Twelve.)
? ? ? ?

If you call a horse's tail a leg, how many legs would he have then? (Still just four. Calling a tail a leg doesn't make it one.)
? ? ? ?

36

If a worm got invited to a picnic in a corn-field, what would he do? (Go in one ear and out the other.)

????

How long is a piece of string? (Twice the distance from the middle to one end.)

????

What do people in Missoula, Montana, call little brown dogs? (Puppies. Same as everywhere else.)

????

How can the city fathers be certain your town's water supply is healthful? (They should use only well water.)

????

What is a sure way of keeping milk from going sour? (Leave it in the cow.)

????

A donkey is tied to a tree with a fifteen-foot rope. Twenty feet away is a bale of hay. The donkey tried and tried to get to the hay. What did he do? (Encourage your victim to suggest various ways, none of which will be logical. Finally, you say, "Do you give up?" When the victim says, "Yes," you reply, "So did the other donkey.")

????

What is Smokey the Bear's middle name? (the)

????

Why isn't your nose twelve inches long?
(Because then it would be a foot.)

? ? ? ?

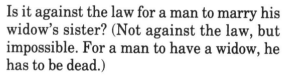

How far can a dog run into the woods?
(Only halfway, because then he's running
out of the woods.)

? ? ? ?

When was milk the highest? (When the
cow jumped over the moon.)

? ? ? ?

Is it against the law for a man to marry his
widow's sister? (Not against the law, but
impossible. For a man to have a widow, he
has to be dead.)

? ? ? ?

You have two coins that add up to fifty-five cents. One of
them is not a nickel. What are the two coins? (A nickel
and a fifty-cent piece. *One* of the coins is not a nickel but
the other one is.)

? ? ? ?

How would an archaeologist who finds a coin marked 525
B.C. know it was a phony? (No one could have known
Christ was going to be born 525 years before the fact.)

? ? ? ?

Do they have the Fourth of July in England? (Of course.
They just don't celebrate it as we do.)

? ? ? ?

38

What date is a military command? (March 4th!)

???? ?

How many of each animal did Moses take into the ark? (Moses didn't take any animals into the ark. That was Noah.)

???? ?

If you only have two sticks, how can you build a fire? (Make sure one of the sticks is a match.)

???? ?

When you need to go to the dentist, what time is it? (2:30. Tooth hurty.)

???? ?

How many birthdays does the average person have? (Just one.)

???? ?

How can you drop a fresh egg six feet without breaking it? (Drop it from a seven-foot ladder. For the first six feet, the egg will be fine. That last foot will be the killer.)

SO FAR, SO GOOD!

???? ?

What is the closest planet to us at the present time? (The earth. It's right under our feet.)

???? ?

Mary Rose sat on a tack. What did she do?
(Mary rose.)

? ? ? ?

If you have only one match, and you enter
a room in which there is a candle, a kero-
sene lamp, and a woodstove, which would
you light first? (You'd better light the
match.)

? ? ? ?

If you take two oranges from three oranges, what would
you have? (You would have two oranges. Isn't that what
you took?)

? ? ? ?

I'll bet you can't say this three times: "Meat without
cheese." (After your victim has said "Meat without
cheese" many times and you have told him he is wrong,
inform him that he should just be saying, "Meat, meat,
meat." That's meat, without cheese.)

? ? ? ?

Do you know how long cows should be
milked?" (Just the same way as short
cows.)

? ? ? ?

Why were the snakes crying when Noah
told them to go forth and multiply? (They
were adders.)

? ? ? ?

Try this one on your preacher — if he has a sense of humor. Have you read all seventeen chapters in the book of Mark? (If he says "Yes," you have a "gotcha." There are only sixteen chapters in the book of Mark.)

????

Make a deal with your victim. If either one asks a question he can't answer himself, he has to be the other's servant for a day.

You ask the first question: When a groundhog digs a hole, why doesn't it leave a pile of dirt around the entrance?

Your victim: I don't know. It's your question. You have to answer it.

You: He starts digging his hole at the other end, that's why.

Victim: How could he get to the other end to start digging?

You: That's your question. You answer it or else, kneel, servant!

????

I walked up the hill and counted fifty windows on my right. I turned around, and on my way back down the hill, I counted fifty windows on my left. How many windows did I count in all? (Fifty windows. The windows on your left going down were the same windows you counted on your right going up.)

????

Not and Shot fought a duel.
Not was shot, and Shot was not.
Would you rather be Shot or Not?
(Answer: I'd rather be Shot. For Not was shot.)

????

41

Would you rather be dumber than you look, or look dumber than you are? (Answer: In either case, you declare it to be impossible.)

? ? ? ?

A man had seven daughters, and each daughter had a brother. How many children did he have in all? (He had eight children. Each daughter had the same brother.)

? ? ? ?

If a farmer raises 200 bushels of corn in dry weather, what does he raise in wet weather? (An umbrella.)

? ? ? ?

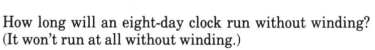

How many times can 19 be subtracted from 190? (Only once. After the first 19 is taken away, you don't have 190 anymore.)

? ? ? ?

How long will an eight-day clock run without winding? (It won't run at all without winding.)

? ? ? ?

What is the last thing you take off at night? (Your feet off the floor.)

? ? ? ?

Do you know why Robin Hood robbed only the rich? (Sure. The poor had no money.)

? ? ? ?

Why is George Washington buried at Mount Vernon? (He is dead.)

? ? ? ?

42

If a boy found a dollar in every pocket in his pants, what would he probably have? (He'd probably have on someone else's pants.)

?????

Why are people so tired on April 1st? (They have just finished a March of 31 days.)

?????

Is it safe to write a letter on an empty stomach? (It's safe enough, but wouldn't it be better to write it on paper?)

?????

If your peacock laid eggs on your neighbor's yard, who could claim ownership of them? (Peacocks don't lay eggs. Peahens do.)

?????

If you crawled into a hole bored all the way through the earth, where would you come out? (Out of the hole.)

?????

Which is better, an old five-dollar bill or a new one? (Any five-dollar bill is better than a one-dollar bill.)

?????

Why is a dog dressed warmer in summer than in winter? (In winter, he wears a fur coat. In summer, he wears the same coat, and pants.)

?????

43

If you add a father, a mother, and a baby, what do you get? (Two and one to carry. A similar "gotcha" is: How does a dog with a hurt leg make an arithmetic problem? He has three and one to carry.)

? ? ? ?

If you can buy six eggs for twenty-six cents, how many can you buy for a cent and a quarter? (The same six. A cent and a quarter equal twenty-six cents.)

? ? ? ?

Did you hear the one about two holes in the ground? (Well, well.)

? ? ? ?

If a dog lost his tail, where should he go? (To a big store where they retail everything.)

? ? ? ?

What is the difference between a sigh and a monkey? (A sigh means, O dear, and a monkey means U, dear.)

? ? ? ?

A man's two horses disappeared. When he found them, they were in a cornfield. One was facing north and the other south, but they could see each other. How could this be? (They were facing each other.)

? ? ? ?

A squirrel found six ears of corn in a hollow tree. If he was only able to carry three ears out at a time, how many trips will he have to make to take the corn to his nest? (Six trips. He can only carry one ear of corn at a time. The other two ears are his own, on his head.)

? ? ? ?

44

What happened in 1492?
(Columbus discovered America.)
Right. What happened in 1500?
(Nothing that I know of.)
Wrong. America had its eighth birthday.

????

When rain falls, does it ever get up again? (In due (dew) time.)

????

Why do firemen wear red suspenders? (To hold up their pants.)

????

Why does an Indian chief wear feathers in his hair? (To keep his wigwam [wig warm]).

????

If joy is the opposite of sorrow, what is the opposite of woe? (Giddyap!)

????

What were the highest mountains in the world before the Alps were discovered? (The Alps. They just hadn't been discovered yet.)

????

Tires hold up cars. What holds up airplanes? (Hijackers.)

????

What does a hen do just before she stands on one leg? (Lifts up the other one.)

????

45

What do you call a person who doesn't have all his fingers on one hand? (Normal. Most of us have fingers on both hands.)

????

What countries are on the other side of the Jordan River? (It depends on which side of the river you're on.)

????

A little girl told the teacher she was seven on her last birthday and would be nine on her next birthday. How could that be true? (That very day was her eighth birthday.)

????

Can you tell me how much water, to a quart, flows through the Mississippi River in a day? (There are two pints in a quart, no matter where it is.)

????

Why does a stork stand on one leg? (If he held up both legs, he'd fall down.)

????

I came to town and met three people. They were neither men, women, nor children. What were they? (A man, a woman, and a child.)

????

If you were riding on a donkey, what fruit would the two of you resemble? (A pear [pair]).

????

February brings the snow;
March brings the winds that blow;
April brings the gentle showers;
What do May flowers bring?
(Pilgrims.)

????

What must you do before getting off a merry-go-round?
(Get on it.)

????

What is the ugliest tree in the world? (Yew [you].)

????

How can you keep water from coming into your house?
(Don't pay the water bill.)

????

If you go to the hardware store for fifty cents worth of
tacks, what do you want them for? (For fifty cents, of
course.)

????

Why should you never try to sweep out a room? (It's too
big a job for you. Just sweep out the dirt, and leave the
room there.)

????

GOTCHAS FOR A GROUP

These "gotchas" work best when done with several people. They are fun to do at parties or anywhere a group has gathered for a good time. Some of them are aimed to "get" one person; some are after the whole group. You must know your part well to make them work, and sometimes, even then, they don't. Then you have to take the "gotcha" on yourself, with grace.

That's Good; That's Bad

The group is instructed to say, together, "Oh, that's good!" after your first sentence; "Oh, that's bad!" after the next, and continue the pattern until the end.

You: Two men went up for a ride in an airplane.

Group: Oh, that's good!

You: No, that's bad. The engine conked out.

Group: Oh, that's bad!

You: No, that's good. They both had parachutes.

Group: Oh, that's good!

You: No, that's bad. The parachutes didn't open.

Group: Oh, that's bad!

You: No, that's good. There was a haystack directly beneath them.

Group: Oh, that's good!

You: No, that's bad. There was a pitchfork in the haystack.

Group: Oh, that's bad!

You: No, that's good. They missed the pitchfork.

Group: Oh, that's good!

You: No, that's bad. They also missed the haystack.

Zap!

Will and Bill

Once upon a time, there were two identical twins named Bill and Will. No one could tell them apart, except that Bill was much smarter than Will. One day, Will went into a neighboring country and was captured by soldiers and taken before the king. Since he had done nothing wrong, Will begged the king for mercy.

The king said, "Very well. I will ask you three riddles and give you one night to think of the answers. If tomorrow, you can tell me the answers, I will set you free. If not, you will be thrown into prison. Here are the riddles: How deep is the ocean? How many balls of string does it take to reach the moon? And what am I thinking? Now, go, and return in the morning."

Meanwhile, Bill had heard of his brother's plight, and got himself smuggled into the prison cell. There, he changed clothes with Will, who slipped away to safety.

The next morning, Bill went before the king.

"How deep is the ocean?" asked the king.

"As deep as a stone's throw," answered Bill. "If you toss a stone into the ocean, it will sink to the bottom."

"Very good," said the king. "Now, how many balls of string does it take to reach the moon?"

"Only one, if it is long enough," answered Bill.

"You have answered two riddles, but this is the hardest one. What am I thinking?" asked the king.

When Bill answered, the king had to let him go. What was the answer?

"You are thinking I am my identical twin, Will," Bill answered.

Zap!

The Jumping Flea

You appear before the group with your left hand cupped as though you were holding something. You say, "I caught this little flea the other day, and have discovered he is a very talented fellow. He can jump several feet into the air, and land back in my hand again. I have grown very fond of him. In fact, I had him some little shoes made out of red velvet that he loves to wear. Would you like to see him jump?

50

If the group indicates that they would, you lean down to your hand and ask very softly, "Will you do your jumping act for my friends?" Act as if you are listening, nodding your head.

"He told me he can't jump as high with his little velvet shoes on, so he's taking them off."

Lean over your hand again, and pretend to pick up a tiny pair of shoes with the fingertips of your right hand. Tell someone at the front of the group to hold out his hand, and pretend to put the shoes in his hand.

"Now, he's ready to jump. You do believe I have a trained flea in my hand, don't you?"

If the person "holding the shoes" says he does not, then you say, "Then how come you're holding his little velvet shoes?"

Zap!

Betty Boop

You tell the group that you are going to ask them to do something together that is almost impossible. All together, they are to say, "Betty Boop, Betty Boop, Betty Boop" over and over again, at least ten times without stopping.

Once they get going with enthusiasm, at about the fifth or sixth "Betty Boop," you swing your arm in a circle over your head as if you were holding a ten-gallon hat aloft, a la the Lone Ranger, and shout, "Hi-yo, Silver! Away!"

Zap!

The Never-ending Tale (No. 1)

Say to the group that you are going to tell them a story that demands complete quiet. Warn them that it will be rude to break the spell of the story by speaking.

It was a dark and stormy night. Some cowboys were sitting around the campfire. Tex said, "Tell us a story, Joe." Joe rose and said, "It was a dark and stormy night.

Some cowboys were sitting around the campfire. Tex said, 'Tell us a story, Joe.' Joe rose and said . . ."

Keep going until someone in the group finally says something.

Zap!

The Never-ending Tale (No. 2)

You will need an accomplice for this one. You will hold this conversation in front of the group.

You: That's tough.

Friend: What's tough?

You: Life.

Friend: What's life?

You: A magazine.

Friend: Where do you get it?

You: A newsstand.

Friend: How much?

You: Fifty cents.

Friend: I only have a quarter.

You: That's tough.

Friend: What's tough?

You continue until someone interrupts. Then you say, "How rude and thoughtless to interrupt a conversation." The risk in this kind of "gotcha" is that the group will let you go on and on until you have to stop.

Zap!

The Sculptor

For this "gotcha" you will need two accomplices and several volunteers from the group to take part. One of the accomplices is seated in a chair, and the volunteers are put into another room so that they can neither see nor hear what is going on.

Bring in one volunteer and say to him, "You are a sculptor. We have here (indicating accomplices) two lumps of clay. You are going to make them into a statue, placing them in any position you desire."

The victim will usually set to work with glee, placing the two accomplices in a romantic position, one on the other's lap, etc. This will be done in the spirit of fun, and in good taste.

When the sculptor is finished, you ask, "Are you done? Is this the way you want the statue to look?" When he replies that it is, ask again, "Are you sure?" He is sure.

Then you say, "All right, you take the place of this statue."

The amount of embarrassment on the part of the victim will depend upon his enthusiasm for romance in his artistic work. When he is arranged as a part of the statue, the replaced accomplice sits down with the group, and another victim is called in. The performance is repeated.

Zap!

Rabbits

Try this one on a friend — perhaps a teacher or counselor — who is beginning to lose his hair, and *who has a sense of humor.*

Ask any number of volunteers to come up front and form a long line. Tell them to take one step backward. Then, ask the victim what the group represents. He will make one or two guesses which will be wrong, of course.

Then, you say, "Pretend these people up here are rabbits." Have them take another step backward, and then another, and ask the victim again what they represent. When he gives up, you say, "This is a receding hare (hair) line."

Zap!

More Rabbits

Since we are on the subject of rabbits, this would be a good place to put in an appropriate knock-knock. Not many of these have been included because they are so numerous (like rabbits) that whole books could be, and have been, written on just this form of humor. So, one knock-knock.

You: Knock-knock.
Group: Who's there?
You: Ether.
Group: Ether who?
You: Ether Bunny.

You: Knock-knock.
Group: Who's there?
You: Samoa.
Group: Samoa who?
You: Samoa Ether Bunnies.

You: Knock-knock.
Group: Who's there?
You: Estelle.
Group: Estelle who?
You: Estelle more Ether Bunnies.

You: Knock-knock.
Group: Who's there?
You: Consumption.
Group: Consumption who?
You: Consumption be done about all these Ether Bunnies?

Zap!

Going to the Movies

See if the group can figure out this one. A duck, a frog, and a skunk went to the movies. Tickets were a dollar. Which got in, and which didn't?

The frog got in. He had a greenback.

The duck got in. He had a bill.

The skunk didn't make it. All he had was a scent (cent), and it was bad.

Zap!

Firefighters

Try this one on the group.

> You: Why do ducks have flat feet?
>   (Answer: To stamp out forest fires.)
> You: Then why do elephants have flat feet?
>   (Someone from the group will probably answer that it's for them to stamp out forest fires too)
> You: Wrong! (Answer: To stamp out burning ducks.)

Zap!

Old Molly Maguire

You: Old Molly Maguire died.
Group: How did she die?
You: Heaving a sigh.
(Everyone heaves a big sigh.)
You: Old Molly Maguire died.
Group: How did she die?
You: Heaving a sigh, and winking one eye.
(Everyone heaves a big sigh and winks one eye. Keep doing this as the gag continues.)
You: Old Molly Maguire died.
Group: How did she die?
You: Heaving a sigh, winking one eye, and her face all awry.
(Everyone heaves a sigh, winks one eye, and makes an ugly face.)
You: Old Molly Maguire died.
Group: How did she die?
You: Heaving a sigh, winking one eye, face all awry, and one foot up high.
(Everyone heaves a sigh, winks one eye, makes an ugly face, and lifts one foot up off the floor.)

You: Old Molly Maguire died.

Group: How did she die?

You: Heaving a sigh, winking one eye, face all awry, one foot up high, and waving goodbye.

(Everyone heaves a sigh, winks one eye, makes a face, lifts one foot off the floor, and waves goodbye.)

Once you have them all involved in this ridiculous-looking series of actions, you make your exit, waving a BIG goodbye.

Zap!

The Court Jester

See if the group can solve this one. A court jester made his king angry, and was condemned to die. The king felt badly about it, however, for the jester had served him long and well and had made him happy on many a day.

"You have been a good fool," the king said to the jester. "But I have condemned you to die, and so it must be. I will, however, grant you a last wish. You may choose the way in which you are to die."

After much thought, the jester, who was truly no fool, came up with an answer which was quite satisfactory. What was it?

(Answer: He chose to die of old age.)

Zap!

The Original Play

Announce to the group that you have written a play and would like to enlist the help of some of them to give it a first run-through. Call for volunteers, and let as many as care to join you at the front come up and stand together. Once you have as many victims as you wish, you announce the name of your play: "A Gathering of Nuts."

Zap!

The Bigger Family

Once upon a time there was a family by the name of Bigger. The family members were Father Bigger, Mother Bigger, Little Johnny Bigger, and Uncle Billy Bigger. Listen carefully, now, and see if you can answer my questions.

The family went to the movies and sat down in this order: Father Bigger, Mother Bigger, Little Johnny Bigger, and Uncle Billy Bigger. Which is the Bigger?

(Answer: Mother Bigger, because she was by far the Bigger — Father Bigger.)

Uncle Billy went on a journey. Now, which is the Bigger?

(Answer: Uncle Billy, because he is by far the Bigger.)

Mother Bigger and Little Johnny Bigger went to the store. Mother Bigger went to buy groceries while Little Johnny Bigger stayed by the pickle barrel. Who was the Bigger?

(Answer: Little Johnny, because he was by a barrel Bigger.)

Father Bigger died. Now, who is the Bigger?

(Father Bigger because he is still Bigger.)

Mother Bigger married Uncle Jerry Bigger. Now, who is the Bigger?

(Answer: Mother Bigger, because she is twice Bigger.)

Zap!

How Many Wives

Ask the group how many wives a man may legally have. When they answer "One," tell them they are wrong. He may have sixteen.

(Proof: It's in the marriage ceremony, "For better, for worse, for richer, for poorer. Pronounce it "Four" better, etc.)

Zap!

The Hound Pup

Once there was a hound pup named August. He was always jumping up on everyone and everything. One day he made the mistake of jumping on the wrong end of a mule. How do we know from this story that the next day was September 1st?

(Answer: Because that was the end of August.)

Zap!

The Power of Suggestion

Ask the group to pronounce, all together, the word "T-o." Then ask them to pronounce, "T-w-o." Now "T-o-o."

Now, what is the second day of the week?

(Almost invariably, the answer will be Tuesday, when the second day of the week is really Monday. The power of suggestion strikes again!)

Zap!

A Very, Very Oldie

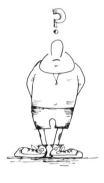

This is one of the oldest group "got-chas," and in today's hurried society, it may not work. One or two members of the group will go to a busy street corner down-town, and start looking up, as if they can see something very strange or interesting in the sky. As prearranged, other members of the group will drift up and join them, and there can even be some pointing and open mouths. Pretty soon, other people will begin to join the group, and before long, you may have drawn a crowd. That's when the original sky-watchers should begin to drift away, leaving some very puzzled people on the corner, wondering what on earth had been so interesting in the sky to attract so many gawkers.

Zap!

A Message With Letters

Write the following letters on a board or have them printed on a placard, and ask the group if they can read the message:

> YY I M
> YY I B
> I C I M
> YY 4 THEE.

(Too wise I am; Too wise I be. I see I am too wise for thee.)

Zap!

Microphone Technique

Ask for someone in the group who would like to improve his speaking technique at the microphone to come forward. Go through the motions of tapping the mike, etc. to make sure it is working.

You: Please stand very close to the mike and say, "Testing, testing, one-two-three."

Victim: Testing, testing, one-two-three.

You: (to group) How does he sound?

Group: Too loud!

You: Move back a step or two, and repeat the testing sentence. (Repeat this procedure several times, with someone in the group who is in on the stunt always declaring that it is still too loud. Finally, the victim is some distance away from the mike.)

You: Say the sentence one more time.

Victim: Testing, testing, one-two-three.

You: (to group) How does it sound now?

Group: We can't hear him.

You: Good. That's the improvement we were looking for.

Zap!

The Barnyard Game

This "gotcha" has to be pre-planned, with everyone in the group but the victim in on the gag.

You: Tonight, we're going to play the barnyard game. I am going around to each one of you and will whisper the name of a barnyard animal in your ear. Then, when I say, "Sound off!" everyone will stand up and make the sound your animal makes at the top of his voice. The one of you who does the best job will be proclaimed "King of the Barnyard" and win a prize.

You go around and pretend to whisper the name of an animal in each person's ear. In reality, they are reminded to remain seated and be perfectly quiet. The victim is the only one given an animal — a donkey, of course.

At the signal, "Sound off!" the victim will stand up and "Hee-haw" loudly, all by himself. If you want to carry the gag a bit farther, you can give him a bag of oats for a prize.

Zap!

Magic Act

You: I have the gift of ESP. If someone in here doesn't believe me, I'll prove it to you.

Victim: You'll have to convince me.

You: Please step up here beside me. Now, reach into your pocket and bring out a coin, any coin. Hold it out toward me in your closed fist. Do you believe I can tell you the date?

Victim: No, I don't. What is it?

You: (Name the date of that day. You didn't say you could tell him the date *of the coin,* only the date.)

Zap!

ONE-LINER "GOTCHAS"

You would never be mean enough to use these "gotchas" except as a comeback to someone who has tried to put you down. (Would you?) Instead of just standing there and saying, lamely, "Oh, yeah?" which is a rather weak reply and has definitely been used before, you add a "gotcha" that should cause your tormentor to slink away, defeated.

This type of "gotcha" sort of dates itself. For instance, in the twenties, a popular one was, "So's your old man!" During World War II, a much-used comeback was "Your mama wears army boots!" A real classic is "Sticks and stones may break my bones, but words will never hurt me." Television recently dredged up this oldie: "I'm rubber and you're glue. What you say bounces off me and sticks to you."

The "gotchas" in this chapter are more of our time, and perhaps new enough to have some shock value. Perhaps they'll work for you. Remember, they usually follow, "Oh, yeah?"

Every time it rains, I think of you — drip, drip, drip.

_____

When you go to school, the teacher plays hooky.

_____

When I want your opinion, I'll give it to you.

_____

I don't know what I'd do without you, but I'm willing to try.

_____

Someday, you'll go too far, and I hope you stay there.

_____

If you played a game of hide-and-seek, nobody would look for you.
_____

You're so fat that when you sit around the
house, you sit *around the house*.
_____

You're so disagreeable that if you threw a boomerang, it
wouldn't come back.
_____

I'd like to say something nice about you, but I can't think
of anything.
_____

You're so dumb you think toothpaste is for people with
loose teeth.
_____

If you're longing for wide-open spaces, try looking between your ears.
_____

You're get-up-and-go has got up and went.
_____

A day away from you is like a month in the country.
_____

In an ugly face contest, you'd win even if you didn't enter.
_____

Some faces stop clocks. Yours starts them running backward.
_____

You're a real peach; you've got a heart of stone.
_____

You're so short that when you sit down and stand up, you're the same size.

———————

I heard you had a lousy personality, but that's not true. You have no personality at all.

———————

The more I think of you, the less I think of you.

———————

Just because your head is shaped like an air-conditioner doesn't mean you're cool.

———————

Roses are red, violets are blue, God made me beautiful, what happened to you?

———————

On you, brain surgery would be a minor operation.

———————

Don't go away mad. Just go away.

———————

I'll be glad to help you out. Which way did you come in?

———————

Do you have a chip on your shoulder, or is that your head?

———————

When you get an idea, it dies in solitary confinement.

———————

At least you'll never be lonely. You have a split personality.

———————

Make like a pair of scissors and cut out.

———————

I can't understand why a two-faced person like you is wearing that one.

———————————

I have an Excedrin headache, and it's just your size.

———————————

You look like an accident going somewhere to happen.

———————————

Go ahead, be as rotten as everyone says you are.

———————————

Your voice just fills the hall. Several people left to make room for it.

———————————

You're so dumb that when you see a Man Wanted poster in the post office, you go in and apply for the job.

———————————

If there's a price on your head, take it.

———————————

You're a one-person slum.

———————————

Arguing with you is like trying to blow out an electric light bulb.

———————————

You're just like London — always in a fog.

Your face looks like a cake that's been left out in the rain.

———————————

Roses are red, violets are blue,
Umbrellas get lost, so why don't you?

———————————

65

You have a mind like Webster, and a head
like Clay.

_____

You look like an unmade bed.

_____

You always have something you can count on — your fingers.

_____

Last night as you lay on your pillow,
Last night as you lay on your bed,
You stuck your feet out of the window;
Next morning, the neighbors were dead!

_____

Your new dress is very smart. I had one
just like it last year.

_____

Don't give me a piece of your mind; you can't spare it.

_____

You're so hard to get along with, you'd give
a cannibal indigestion.

_____

You take a long time making up your mind
because you're short of material.

_____

You're so dumb you think a case of diphtheria is something to drink.

_____

You're so dull you get bored talking to yourself.

_____

You have an even disposition — always sour.

_____

You should be on the stage. There's one leaving in half an hour.

_____

You're so modest you have to leave the room to change your mind.

_____

You're built upside down: your nose runs and your feet smell.

_____

Make like the wind, and blow!

_____

Who does your hair, the Bride of Frankenstein?

_____

I'll admit you're stronger than I am, but bad breath isn't everything.

_____

Is that your head, or did someone discover a way to grow hair on a meatball?

_____

How can you be here? I thought all dodo birds were extinct.

_____

Why don't you make like a desert, and dry up?

_____

You think you're a real dreamboat, but you're really just a shipwreck.

_____

67

What put you in such a bad mood today? Did you get up on the wrong side of your cage?

_____

I've seen better hairdos on mops.

_____

How did you manage to live through Thanksgiving?

_____

I heard you went to the doctor yesterday. Did your vet find anything wrong?

_____

I saw your picture in the papers the other day — the funny papers.

_____

Run and hide, quick! Here comes a buzzard!

_____

If your face is your fortune, you'll never have to pay income tax.

_____

You're so clumsy that if you fell down, you'd probably miss the floor.

_____

When I see you, I think of the sea. You really make me sick.

_____

On the tree trunk of life, you're nothing but a knothole.

_____

You're so dumb that when you go window shopping, you buy windows.

_____

68

When you talk to your house plants, they wilt.

_____

If you kissed a prince, he'd probably turn into a frog.

_____

You're so dumb you think they sell fleas at a flea market.

_____

You're such a loser that M&M's melt in your hand.

_____

If I had a face like yours, I'd hire a burglar to steal it.

_____

Your name may not be in WHO's WHO, but I betcha it's in WHAT'S THIS?

_____

You're so ugly that when a tear rolls down your face, it rolls right back up again.

_____

Go ahead and enjoy yourself. After all, you have nine lives to live.

_____

You need to watch your waistline, and aren't you lucky that it's right out there where you can?

_____

You're such a loser that if it was raining soup, you'd be standing outside with a fork.

_____

Your face is like a flower — a cauliflower.

_____

There are some "gotchas" that have been around almost since Adam introduced himself to Eve by saying, "Madam, I'm Adam." (That's a palindrome.) Some of them have been quoted in speeches and told at various get-togethers so often that their origins have become fuzzy. For instance, this one has been credited to persons as far apart as Winston Churchill and Dizzy Dean:

Lady Astor became very angry at whoever-it-was at a dinner party, and said to him, "Sir, if I were your wife, I'd put poison in your coffee." To which, whoever-it-was replied, "Madam, if you were my wife, I'd drink it."

Others, like Topsy, seem to have "just growed," and are credited to that very prolific writer, Anonymous. There will be a wide variety of both kinds in this chapter. For our purpose, we will give the originator of the "gotcha" credit when we know it. Otherwise, it will be considered anonymous.

I never forget a face, but in your case, I'll make an exception.

— Groucho Marx

Pick: I have an idea.
Pat: Treat it kindly. It's in a strange place.

Your teeth are just like stars. They come out at night.

A note to the track team: Verily, the sap runneth in the spring.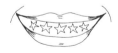

It is better to keep one's mouth closed and be thought a fool, than to open it and remove all doubt.

— Abraham Lincoln

Mom: Why don't you answer the phone?
Kid: It isn't ringing.
Mom: That's just like you to wait until the last minute.

71

1st Englishman: Sorry to hear you buried your wife.
2nd Englishman: Had to. Dead, you know.

Oh, wad some power the giftie gie us
To see oursels as others see us!
— Robert Burns

At one time, Mark Twain went to a neighbor's house to borrow a book. "I'll be glad to let you use it," said the neighbor. "But it's a rule I have that my books must be read right here in my house." A few days later, this same neighbor went over to borrow Twain's lawnmower. He was told, "Sure, you can use it. But it's a rule I have that my mower must be used right here in my yard."

You're a poet, but the world don't know it.
Your feet do, though. They're Longfellows.

Man: Call me a cab.
Doorman: Okay. You're a cab.
— Groucho Marx

Student: Teacher, I ain't got no pencil.
Teacher: No, no. I *have* no pencil. She *has* no pencil. You *have* no pencil.
Student: My gosh. Where have all the pencils gone?

Three old ladies who were a little bit hard of hearing met on the street one day.
  1st old lady: My, but it's windy.
  2nd: Oh, no, it's Thursday.
  3rd: Me, too. Let's go get something to drink.

Sherlock Holmes was in his study one night when his friend and assistant, Dr. Watson, came in. After greeting his friend, Holmes said to him, "Don't you think it's a bit warm for you to be wearing your woolen underwear?"

"You never cease to amaze me with your powers of deduction, Holmes," Watson exclaimed. "But how on earth did you figure out that I am wearing woolen underwear?"

"Elementary, my dear Watson," said Holmes. "You forgot to put on your trousers."

The farmer boy, with wistful sigh
Leaned on his hoe and said,
"The fish is bitin' mighty hard
Down at the river, Dad."
The farmer, with a little grin,
Cut down a weed or two.
"Just keep on hoein' 'taters, son,
Them fish, they won't bite you."

The trouble with Shakespeare is you never get to sit down unless you're a king.

— George Kaufman

Father: When Abe Lincoln was your age, he was earning his own living.
Son: And when he was your age, he was president of the United States.

General Hooker was a very energetic leader on the side of the North in the Civil War. He especially liked to make a good impression on others, riding his horse with great flair and giving a great many orders.

At one time, Lincoln received a report from General Hooker which gave the return address as "Headquarters in the Saddle." Lincoln drily remarked, "The trouble

with Hooker is he has his headquarters where his hind-
quarters ought to be."

Mom: I can't believe you're having such a hard time
learning the names of the states. When I was your
age, I could name them in alphabetical order.
Kid: Yeah, but there were only thirteen of them then.

My friend, I agree with you. But what are we two against
so many?

— George Bernard Shaw

Voter: Why, you little pipsqueak! I could swallow you in
one bite.
Douglas: And if you did, you'd have more brains in your
belly than you have in your head.

Your face, you don't mind it,
For you stand behind it;
It's the guy out in front gets the jar.

Son: Dad, what's nuclear fission?
Dad: I really don't know too much about that, son.
Son: What keeps space stations in the air?
Dad: I really can't explain that.
Son: What is a retro-rocket, Dad?
Dad: That's a bit too complicated to explain.
Son: I guess I'm bothering you with all these questions.
Dad: Not at all, son. If you don't ask questions, you'll
never learn anything.

I think I know why you're such a mess.
When the Lord said *head,* you thought he said *bread,*
and asked for yours to be thick and crusty.
When the Lord said *brain,* you thought he said *pain,*
and you told him you didn't care for any.
When the Lord said *ears,* you thought he said *beers,*
and asked for two great big ones.

When the Lord said *nose,* you thought he said *rose,* and told him you'd like a big red one.

When the Lord said *feet,* you thought he said *meat,* and asked for two big hams.

When he was just getting started, Abraham Lincoln was too poor to buy a horse. He had to walk everywhere he went, and sometimes he grew very tired. One hot afternoon he hailed a carriage that was approaching, and when it stopped, he asked the man inside, "Would you mind taking my coat into town?"

"Not at all," replied the man. "But how will you get it back?"

"Oh," replied Lincoln, getting into the carriage. "I'll just stay inside it."

When Jack Benny plays the violin, it sounds like the strings are still in the cat.
— Fred Allen

I've had a wonderful evening, but this wasn't it.
— Groucho Marx

Young man to Mozart: I would like to compose a symphony. Can you give me some advice?
Mozart: You are very young. Why don't you start with ballads?
Young man: But you were composing symphonies when you were ten years old.
Mozart: True. But I didn't ask how.

Once upon a time, there were two little skunks named In and Out. When In was Out, Out was In, and when Out was In, In was Out. One day, Mother Skunk was in the house with Out. She said, "Out, I want you to go out and bring In in." Out went out, and in a very short time, he was back with In. Mother Skunk was amazed. "How

75

were you able to find In so quickly?" she asked. Out replied, "Instinct." (In stinked.)

> Women's faults are many;
> Men have only two:
> Everything they say,
> And everything they do.

Patient: I have a pain in my left leg, Doc.
Doctor: I'm afraid I can't do anything for it. It's just old age.
Patient: But my right leg is just as old, and it doesn't hurt a bit.

"Superman didn't need no seat belt," Muhammad Ali grumbled to the flight attendant who was telling him to buckle up.

To which the young lady retorted, "Superman didn't need no plane neither."

No one could do the "gotcha" better than Shakespeare. A few classic examples:

I thank you for your company; but good faith, I had as lief have been myself alone.
— As You Like It

Out of my sight! Thou dost infect mine eye.
— Richard III

Out, you green-sickness carrion! Out, you baggage! You tallow face!
— Romeo and Juliet

Thou hast pared thy wit o' both sides, and left nothing i' the middle.
— King Lear

God hath given you one face, and you make yourselves another.
— Hamlet

You'll be rotten ere you be half ripe.

— As You Like It

Horace Greeley, a well-known newspaper-man during Civil War days, always insisted that "news" should be a plural noun. At one time, when he was abroad, he cabled his office to ask, "Are there any news?"

The answer he received back from one of his reporters was, "Not a new."

1st salesman: What do you sell?
2nd: Salt.
1st salesman: I'm a salt seller too.
2nd: Shake.

A little boy was sitting on the steps of a house when a salesman came up to him.

"Is your mother at home?" the salesman asked.

"Yep," answered the boy.

The salesman went up and knocked on the door. There was no response from inside the house. He rang the doorbell. Still no one came. After several more tries with no success, he turned around to the little boy.

"If your mother's home, why doesn't she come to the door?" he asked.

"'Cause I don't live here," answered the boy.

The priest asked the little boy if he said his prayers every night. "Not every night," the boy replied. "There's some nights when I don't want anything."

How would you punctuate this sentence: I see a dollar in the street.

Just make a dash after it.

Boy: I et seven eggs for breakfast this morning.
Teacher: You mean ate.
Boy: No. I only et seven.
Teacher: Ate.
Boy: Well, maybe it was eight I et.

Why did the preacher named Tweedle refuse his Doctor of Divinity degree?

He didn't want to be known as Dr. Tweedle, D.D.

Teacher: Correct this sentence: It was me that busted the window.
Student: It wasn't me that busted the window.

Actor W. C. Fields got very angry at a columnist once for reporting that he had died. He called the paper.

"I hope you noticed," he shouted, "that your lousy rag announced my death this morning."

"Yes, I did," replied the editor. "May I ask where you're calling from?"

Big sister: Bobby, if you eat another piece of that pie, you're going to burst.
Bobby: Okay. Pass the pie and get out of the way.

Visitor: Why is your dog watching me so closely while I eat?
Host: Maybe it's because you're eating out of his plate.

Abraham Lincoln was often teased about his height and the length of his legs. A man once asked him what he thought the ideal length should be for a man's legs.

"Just long enough to reach the ground," Abe replied.

Teacher: Let's talk about the grizzly bear. Do we get fur from him?
Kid: I'd get just as fur from him as I possibly could.

Dad: Did you put out the cat?
Son: No. I didn't know it was on fire.

When the Associated Press printed an obituary on Mark Twain, he cabled them from London, as follows: "The reports of my death are greatly exaggerated."

Customer: I would like a pair of alligator shoes.
Salesman: Yes, ma'am. What size is your alligator?

A tourist stopped an old-timer and asked him how far it was to a certain large town. "Wal," said the old man, "if you keep on in the direction your headin', it's about 24,992,601, but if'n you turn around, it's only about 25 miles.

Mother: Eat your spinach, dear. It will put color in your cheeks.
Little girl: But who wants green cheeks?

Mrs. Smith: Will you join me in a cup of tea?
Mrs. Jones: Well, you get in first and I'll see if there's any room left for me.

Salesman: Lady, this mop will do half your work for you.
Housewife: Oh, great! I'll take two of them.

Customer: Waitress, it's been an hour since I ordered some turtle soup.
Waitress: Well, you know how turtles are.

He asked the girl to wed.
She knew that he knew that her father was dead
And she knew that he knew what a wild life he'd led
So she knew that he knew what she meant when she said,
    "Go ask Father."

Teacher: Conjugate the verb "swim."
Student: Swim, swam, swum.
Teacher: Now, conjugate the verb "dim."
Student: Dim — hey, teacher, are you puttin' me on?

Young man: I'm a very good mind reader. I can tell exactly what someone else is thinking.
Young girl: In that case, I beg your pardon.

Bragging mother: Susie is so smart. She's been walking since she was ten months old.
Bored listener: My gosh! Isn't she awfully tired?

Coach: What's the new guy's name?
Manager: Ascowinskiewsky.
Coach: Put him on the 1st team. I hate the newspapers around here.

Boyfriend: I'm so lucky. Here it is a gorgeous night, and I'm out with the most beautiful, the sweetest, the classiest girl in the whole world!
Girlfriend: How you exaggerate. You know it looks like rain.

Same guy: I'll be frank with you. You're not the first girl I ever kissed.
Same gal: And I'll be equally frank with you. You've got a lot to learn.

Prof: If any of you in this class consider yourselves a dumb-bell, please stand up.

Several seconds went by, and then Freshman Jones stood up.

Prof: So, Mr. Jones, do you think you're a dumb-bell?

Freshman Jones: No, sir. But I just hate to see you standing up all by yourself.

Teacher: If "A" has six apples, and "B" has nine apples, how many apples would they have together?

Dumb kid: Why must we go on pretending, pretending, pretending?

A Shakespearian actor was giving his all in a performance of *Richard III*. After he had delivered the line, "A horse! My kingdom for a horse!" a voice came from high up in the gallery, "Could you use a jackass instead?"

Without missing a beat, the actor replied, "Perhaps. Come on down and I'll audition you for the part."

Sir William Gilbert of the light-opera team of Gilbert and Sullivan had a very sour disposition and a bad temper. One day he complained that he was not feeling well. "I have a strange bitter taste in my mouth," he said.

A close friend was quick to suggest, "Perhaps you bit your tongue."

President Calvin Coolidge never had much to say. In fact, when a newspaper reporter was told that he had just died, the reporter asked, "How can they tell?"

At another time, a reporter came up to the president and said, "Mr. President, I made a bet with my editor that I could get you to say more than two words."

"You lose," replied the president.

High-society hostess Mrs. Cornelius Vanderbilt once asked the great violinist Fritz Kreisler how much he would charge to play at one of the big parties in her mansion.

"My standard fee is $18,000," Kreisler told her.

"Very well," replied the lady. "But I'm sure you understand that you are not to mingle with the guests."

"Oh," said the violinist, "in that case, my fee is only $10,000."

Winston Churchill was a master of the instant put-down — "gotchas" with an English accent. Even after he became quite old, he liked to drop in occasionally at the House of Commons to keep up with affairs. Once, as he was being helped to his seat, two young members of Parliament began whispering about his feeble condition.

"They say, you know," one said, "that he's not only losing his strength of body, but that he's also getting a bit soft in the head."

At which point Churchill turned and fixed them with a steely eye. "They also say," he stated, "that he has become hard-of-hearing."

A young playwright was submitting his work to a producer.

"I can't tell you how hard I've worked on this play," he said. "Night after night, day after day, I've slaved away to make it a work of art."

The producer read a few pages, and then handed the manuscript back to the writer. "What a pity," he murmured. "All that work, and no play."

A group of actresses at a party at the home of Rosalind Russell were discussing their great enemy, growing old.

"I dread the thought of forty-five," said one.

"Why, my dear?" asked Miss Russell. "What happened to you then?"

W. C. Fields was having some drinks at a restaurant. He burped loudly, and a woman at the next table turned and looked at him, horrified.

"What did you expect, madam?" Fields inquired. "Chimes?"

Two children of movie stars whose parents had been married, remarried and divorced many times were having an argument. Finally, one said, "Listen, you better shut up. I'll tell my dad, and my dad can lick your dad."

"Don't be silly," retorted the other. "Your dad *is* my dad."

If silence is golden, you are bankrupt!
— Charlie Chan to talkative No. 1 Son in old movie

EPITAPHS

THE ULTIMATE "GOTCHA"

The ancients believed that if you read epitaphs, you would lose your memory. If that were true, there would be many, many absent-minded folks roaming the world today. The reading of epitaphs in the hope of finding an unusual one has become a hobby with a great number of people.

In theory, epitaphs are a means of saying a last good word about the dearly departed. For some, however, it has become a way of having the last word — sometimes a complimentary and loving one, sometimes not. A few eccentric persons have even written their own, as a parting shot to the world — a final "gotcha." A good example of this is the well-known one that stands at the grave of comedian W. C. Fields: "On the whole, I'd rather be in Philadelphia."

He rocked the boat
Did Ezra Shank
These bubbles mark
o
o
o
o
Where Ezra sank.

Here lies John Yeast
Pardon me for not rising.

Here lies Lester Moore
Four slugs
From a forty-four
No Les
No more

Once I wasn't. Then I was.
Now I ain't again.

85

Ashes to ashes
Dust to dust
In the wrong man
She placed her trust

John Smith is dead, and here he lies.
Nobody laughs and nobody cries.
Where he's gone and how he fares
Nobody knows and nobody cares.

I *told* you I was sick!

Here lies Ann Mann
Who lived an old maid
But died an old Mann
Dec. 8, 1767

Haine
haint

How happy is he I cannot know
But happy am I to see him go!

Here lies
Ezekiel Akles
Aged 102
The Good Die Young

Here lies the body of Susan Jones
Resting beneath these polished stones
Her name was Brown instead of Jones
But Brown won't rhyme with polished stones
And she won't know if it's Brown or Jones.

The Defense Rests

Rose Alice Wise
Clean was her manse
Dust a disgrace
Now here she lies
Dust on her hands
Dust in her face.

Sometimes a postcript is added, a "gotcha gotcha!":
Here lies a lawyer and an honest man
It must be crowded
Two men in one little grave.

A bereaved widow inscribed on her late husband's grave:
The light of my life has gone out
Sometime later, she remarried, and added to the above:
But I have struck another match!

Epitaph suggested by writer Dorothy Parker:
If you can read this
YOU'RE TOO CLOSE!

Tombstone of an atheist:
JAMES JONES
All Dressed Up
and
No Place To Go

N. S.
McGINNIS
FINIS

A FEW GOOD-BYE "GOTCHAS"

Two brothers named Tad and Moe went out for a ride on a pony. The pony threw Moe off. When Tad got home, his mother asked where Moe was. Tad replied, "Tad's all there is. There ain't no Moe." _____

As the monkey said when the lawnmower ran over his tail, "That was the end of me." _____

The doting grandmother said to her little grandson, "Gramma would like to see more of you." The little boy replied, "This is all there is. There isn't any more." _____

You: What is the first letter of "Think"?
Victim: T.
You: Right. What's the first letter of "Quick"?
Victim: Q.
You: Right. Now, can you say both letters together?
Victim: TQ.
You: You're welcome! _____

89

Part One

WHAT'S IT?
Puzzles To Fool the Eye

91

Before you begin

Contrary to the popular saying, what you see is not always what you get. The eye can sometimes lead you astray. In the following pages, what you think you see at first glance may not be what the picture intends at all. Look again, and again, and maybe even a third time. In some cases, the cartoon characters will give you a hint. If you just can't figure it out, the answer will be at the bottom of the page, upside down. (But when you turn the book over, everyone will know you couldn't get the answer by yourself!)

A pig going around the corner of a barn

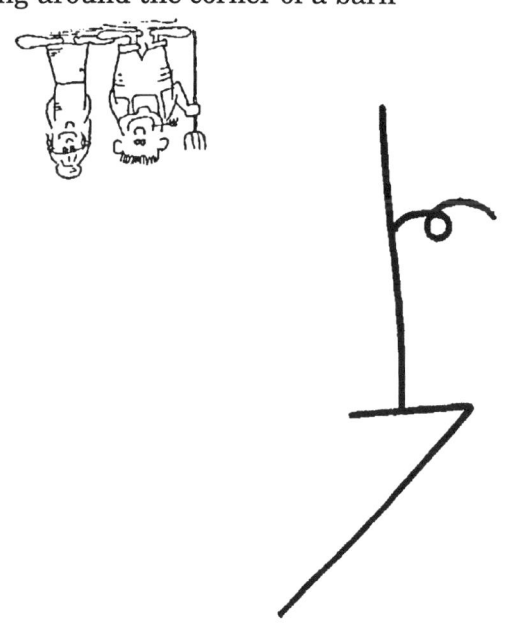

Looking up at a diving board

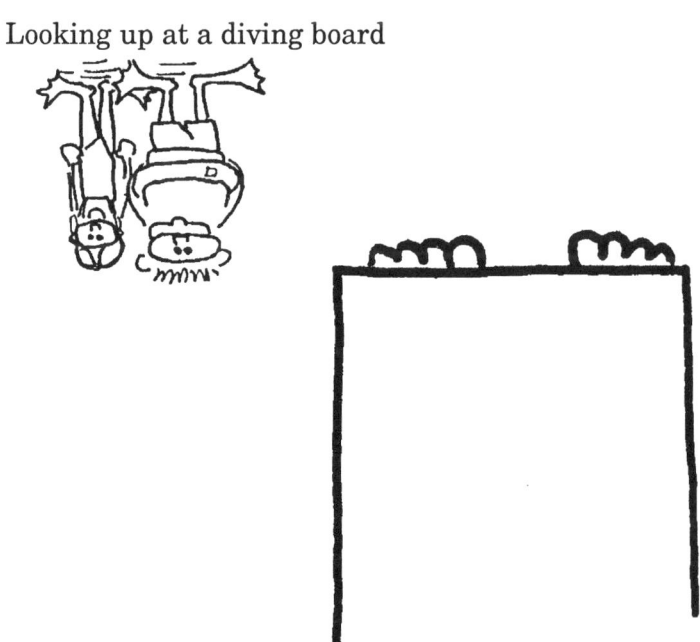

Stepping on a wad of chewing gum

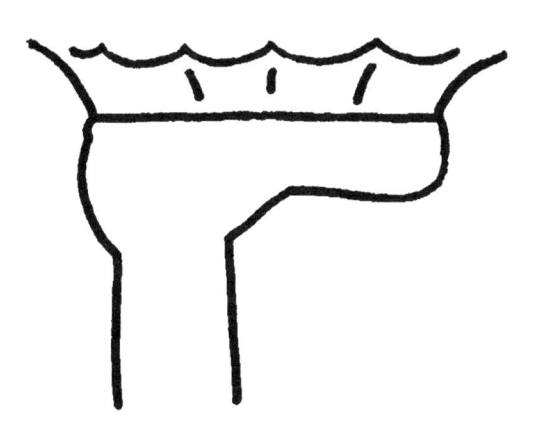

Daddy in the bathtub

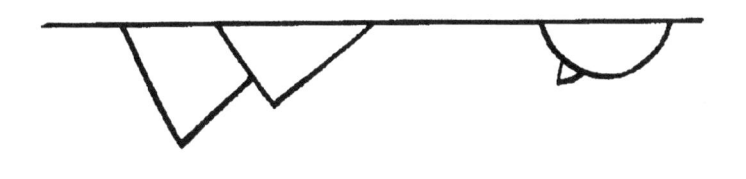

Bird's-eye view of a cowboy frying an egg

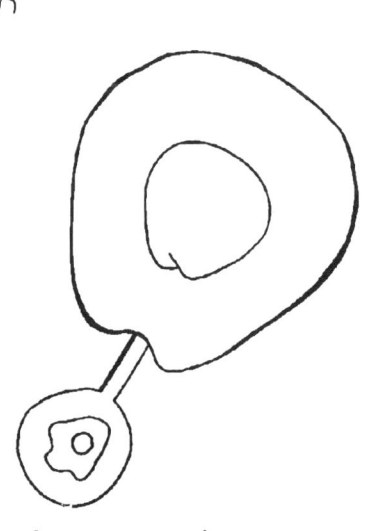

A spider doing push-ups on a mirror

Running up a big bill

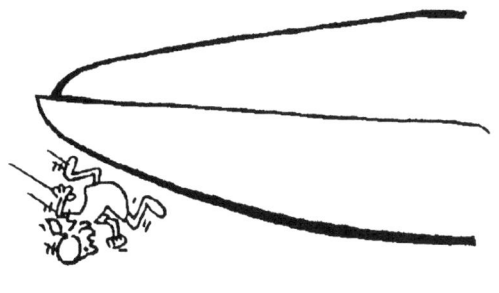

A two-carat ring

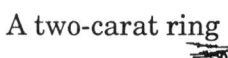

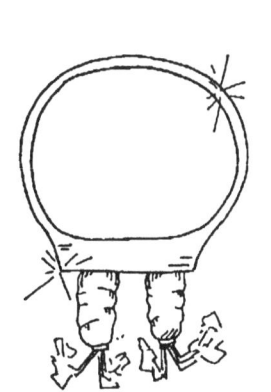

Paris in the spring

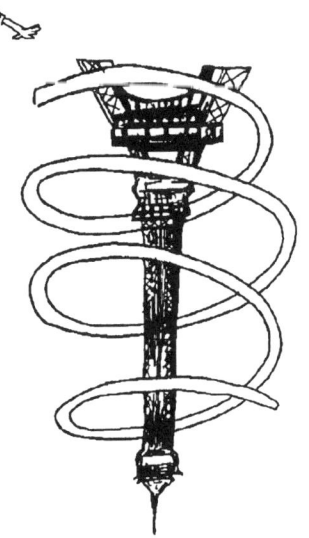

Rear view of a mad cat

Bowling ball for a centipede

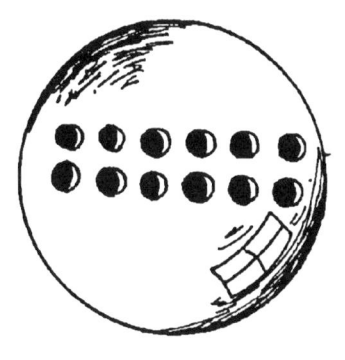

A polar bear in a snowstorm

A bear climbing up the other side of a tree

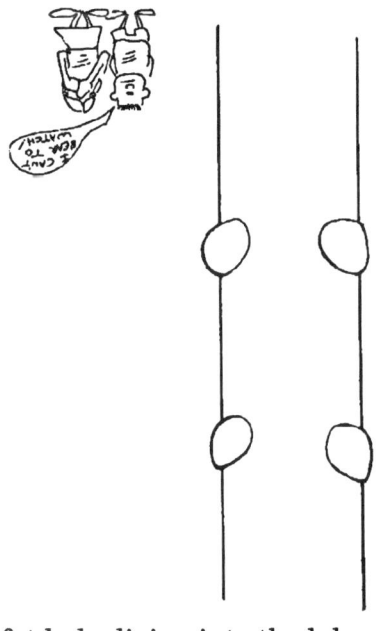

Rear view of a fat lady diving into the lake

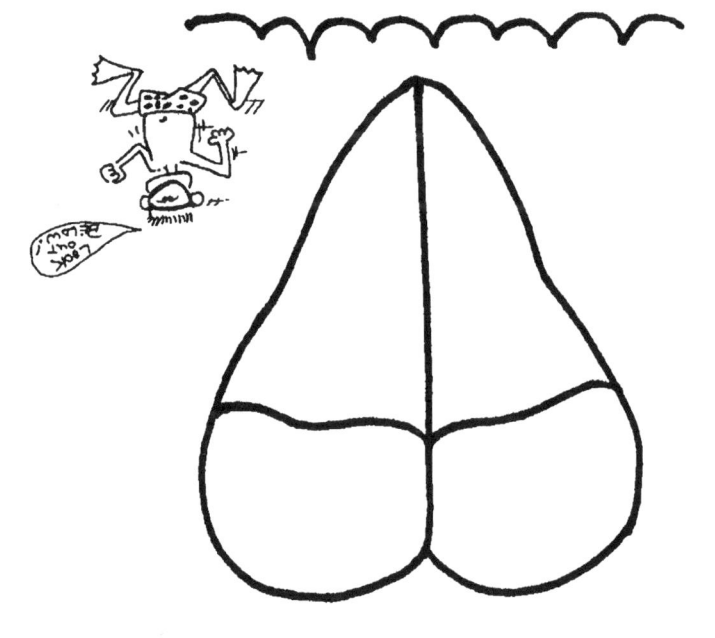

A caterpillar doing a somersault

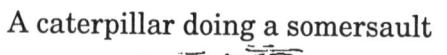

Bird's-eye view of an elephant taking a sunbath

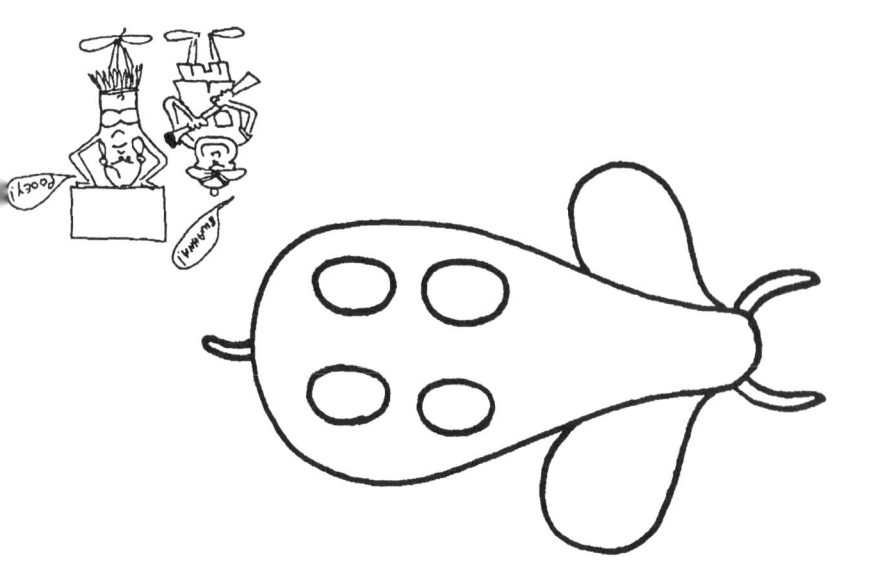

Dueling snails

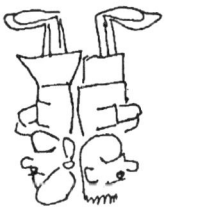

Bubble-gum champ

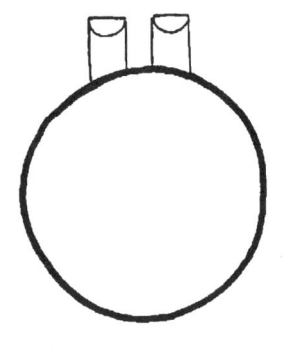

An elephant in the swimming pool

Dracula's toothbrush

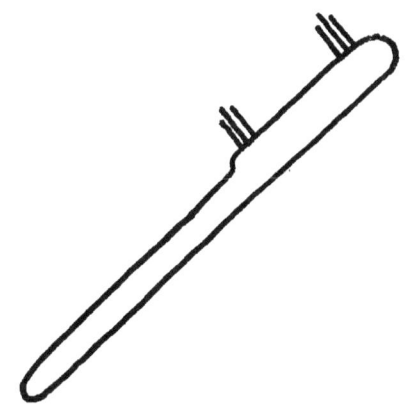

Worm with a hula hoop

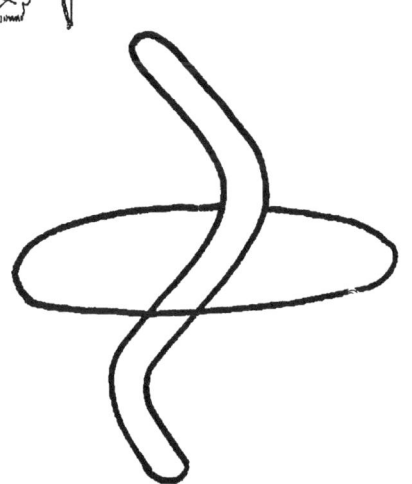

Spectacles for Cyclops

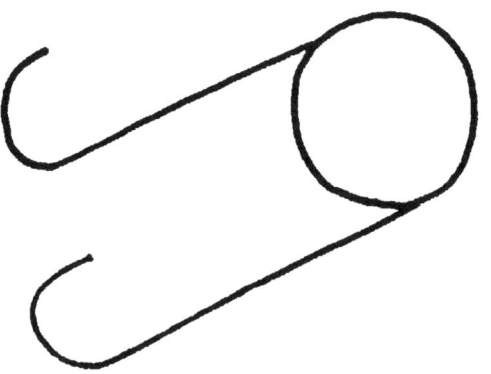

Sandwich at a vampire's picnic

Part Two

WHAT'S IT SAY?
Familiar Words and Phrases in Puzzle Form

105

The check is in the mail

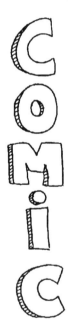

Stand-up comic

GROUND

FEET   FEET

FEET   FEET

FEET   FEET

Six feet under ground

Stone

Cornerstone

Top of the morning

Reading between the lines

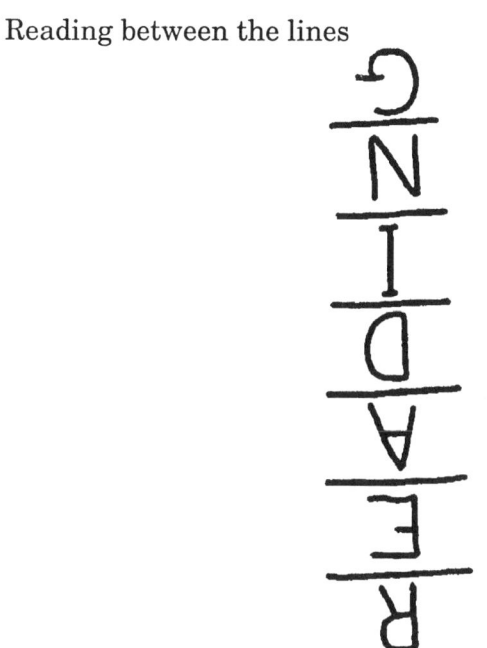

i i i i i i i

O O O O O O O

Circles under the eyes

Weeping willow

JiNK JiNK JiNK JiNK

Highjinks

hair-

Receding hairline

WE AR

LONG

Long underwear

Waving goodbye

I'M—MYSELF

I'm beside myself

M CE

M CE

M CE

Three blind mice

112

C C
GARAGE
R R

VROOM! VROOM!   EEEK!

Two-car garage

HOUSE

PRAIRIE

Little house on the prairie

BLCOUSE

See-through blouse

114

Part Three

WHAT'S IT
— OR IS IT?
Optical Illusions To
Tease the Eye

Is this a lovely young lady looking away from you, or the profile of an ugly old hag?

Is this the head of a bunny, or a duck?

Is the crown of this hat taller than the brim is wide? Measure and see.

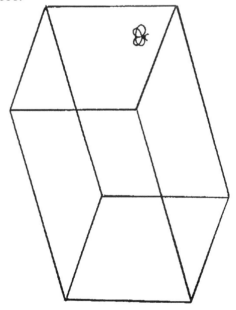

Is the butterfly inside or outside of the box?

Which line is longer? Measure, and be surprised.

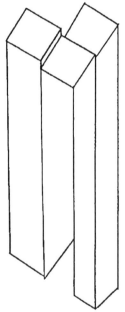

Could you color each of these bars a different color?

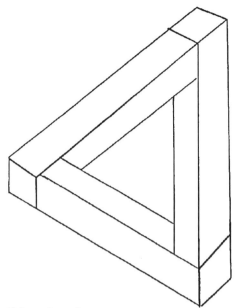

An impossible triangle

Do you see a vase, or two faces staring at each other?